YOUR KNOWLEDGE HAS VALUE

- We will publish your bachelor's and master's thesis, essays and papers

- Your own eBook and book - sold worldwide in all relevant shops

- Earn money with each sale

Upload your text at www.GRIN.com and publish for free

Bibliographic information published by the German National Library:

The German National Library lists this publication in the National Bibliography; detailed bibliographic data are available on the Internet at http://dnb.dnb.de .

Imprint:

Copyright © 2014 GRIN Verlag, Open Publishing GmbH
Print and binding: Books on Demand GmbH, Norderstedt Germany
ISBN: 9783668220690

This book at GRIN:

http://www.grin.com/en/e-book/322898/the-viral-video-phenomenon-what-makes-videos-go-viral

Katja Grasberger

The Viral Video Phenomenon. What makes videos go viral?

GRIN Publishing

GRIN - Your knowledge has value

Since its foundation in 1998, GRIN has specialized in publishing academic texts by students, college teachers and other academics as e-book and printed book. The website www.grin.com is an ideal platform for presenting term papers, final papers, scientific essays, dissertations and specialist books.

Visit us on the internet:

http://www.grin.com/

http://www.facebook.com/grincom

http://www.twitter.com/grin_com

Katja Grasberger

Digital Cultures

27 March 2014

The Viral Video Phenomenon -What Makes videos go viral?

It will probably shock you that the original version of "Gangnam Style" by the Korean singer PSY[1] (standing for psycho) is the most watched video on YouTube of all time counting over 800 million views since it has been uploaded in 2010. What it features is a song that will stick to your head, and dance moves everyone will try to imitate - it had what it took to go "viral", to spread around the world like a sickness. This phenomena is not bound to one specific video genre, in this case a music video, but can be found in other genres as well, for example in comics, animal or amateur videos. Everyone can become famous on the internet by the day after tomorrow if his or her video got what it takes to become viral. But what does it take? A lot of viral videos do not feature informative content that helps us in any way or is important for our lives, nor does the content make any sense at all sometimes. It even appears that the videos with no content are even more popular.

Although there are many viral videos of very different genres, they all share to some degree certain qualities, however can their success in the digital Internet age not be boiled down to a simple set of rules, neither can it be predicted, because these qualities are only features that can help as it has also a lot to do with luck and timing.

By looking at the videos *"Charlie bit my finger - again!"*, *"The Sneezing Baby Panda" and "Dramatic Chipmunk"*, *"David After Dentist"* we will see that although they are very different and feature different content they have qualities that are similar and that some

---

[1] currently not avaible on YouTube in Germany due to GEMA restrictions (20 March 2014)

have qualities that the others will not have, demonstrating that there are no general or universal rules one can use and then have viral success.

VIRAL VIDEO PHENOMENON

When we hear the word "viral" we will first associate it with infectious sicknesses, but when you type in "viral" into Google, you are more likely to encounter "viral" videos. What distinguishes viral videos from other videos is the fact that they were not only watched, but the viewers also felt the need to share them via social websites or e-mails so that on this way it became highly popular throughout the internet.

What constitutes a viral video. What counts as viral is a difficult question, but some years ago videos that gained over 1 million hits on YouTube were generally assumed to be viral. The bigger proportion of videos on YouTube do not get so much attention, more than 50% have less than 500 views (cf Seedwell 2012). Kevin Nalty, a "weblebrity", who is better known as "Nalts", however, claims that 1 million would have been sufficient a few years ago, but he thinks a video is "viral if it gets more than 5 million views in a 3-7 day period." But it is not just the views, Nalts writes "the degree of discussion online and offline (media)" is also decisive (Nalts 2011). It is not only important how many videos get, but moreover that they sticks to the viewers minds and that they will be still talked about in a few years time (cf O'Neill 2011).

Sharing phenomenon. This is not merely a phenomenon of the digital age, viral sharing was already popular 200 years ago, says Professor Cordell who is a digital-media scholar at Northeastern University. The viral culture of 19th century is quite similar to the digital internet culture, but at the same time is totally different (cf Rosen 2013). What was shared in the 19th century were of course no digital images or videos, but rather texts, and the content of these texts share qualities which are similar to the qualities in the media that go viral today. Cordell writes, "Brevity, comedy, charm, and resonance with cultural values (in the 19th century, those were often religious ones)" were all qualities which "increased the likelihood of virality" (cf Rosen 2013). Something new today is the immediacy of electronic media. Whilst earlier you had to pay someone to put the text on the press, today this sharing feature is just one click away and totally for free. There is, however, never a guarantee of sharing.

How do videos become viral? Every minute 40 hours of video footage is uploaded to YouTube and only a tiny percentage becomes viral, says Kevin Allocca who works for YouTube as the trend manager (cf Allocca 2011). Professor Cordell already gave an idea of how videos become viral. It is of course the sharing behavior - what is it that makes people not only watch the video, but also share it with family and friends? Thales S. Teixeira says the best way to attract attention was evoking surprise and the best way of retaining it was to evoke moments of joy (cf Nobel 2013). According to an assistant Professor called Jonah Berger it has to do with visceral emotions certain videos evoke in viewers. If highly aroused we will be more likely to share information, both in awe or anger. Jonah Lehrer, the author of the article, presents Bergers results of previous works in which he analyzed articles which appeared on the most-emailed list and concludes with "we don't want to share facts - we want to share feelings" (Lehrer 2011). This desire has also something to do with solidarity and connectivity. The problem is, Lehrer argues, when online, we have to find a substitute to express our feelings directly as there is mostly no actual face-to-face contact. Lehrer quotes Berger, ". . . sharing content on the Web allows us to get a parallel kind of connection" (Lehrer 2011). Berger und Milkman furthermore found out "that videos that shock or inspire are more likely to be shared on Facebook and more likely to gain viral traction" (cf Konnikova 2014). The quality of the content is also important, as Konnikova quotes Berger, "People love stories. The more you see your story as part of a broader narrative, the better" (Konnikova 2014). Furthermore videos that go viral will feature "good" content staging funny people, especially old people and babies, animals, especially baby animals, dancing and music that gets you involved (cf Miller 2011).

However it is not only all about emotions and physical arousal, Jared Keller argues it is also about culture. First of all viral stories are being shared on platforms like Reddit, 4chan, Facebook, LinkedIn or Twitter and each sharing ecosystem has its own subculture consisting of an own set of rules of orders and norms of behavior. A lot of media companies have tried to put viral sharing behavior into one equation so that they can predict viral success, which could be especially helpful for advertisement. Although technological tools like the Facebook "like" button can help, virality can not be optimized or be reduced to a consistent formula. As Miller claims in her article "creating a video that attracts millions of viewers and becomes a pop culture phenomenon involves an unpredictable cocktail of luck and timing" (Miller 2011). The sharing behavior differs across platforms, which can be seen if one looks at the most popular stories on Twitter[2] and Facebook[3] in 2011. Just because now we have so much of accessible information, does not make us absorb information faster. We now select informations according to our values (cf Keller 2012). Good headlines are therefore also helpful that are short and work as a link bait (cf Konnikova 2014), because this makes them also very easy to find if the viewer only has to remember three to five words.

---

[2] http://yearinreview.twitter.com/en/hottopics.html

[3] http://mashable.com/2011/12/07/facebook-reveals-2011s-most-popular-status-trends/

Furthermore another secret is that of the past: making old things new. Picking up stories that went minor viral and make it even better, because we only know what has worked in the past (cf Thompson 2012). This also holds true for movie industries that created very popular movies, e.g. Saw I, Saw II, Saw III, etc.

It is also the promise of practical value that makes a viewer share, e.g. if you see a Top-10 list of funny cat-memes. It is already put together and selected, so why not share it for the sake of your online-image as well? It might in addition improve the viewer's reputation among friends (cf Nobel 2013).

Kevin Allocca, mentioned above, talks about viral videos in a TED talk and argues that there are three things that make videos go viral: a) Tastemakers b) Communities of participation and c) Unexpectedness. The notion of unexpectedness has already been mentioned as the notion of surprise that will get the attention of the viewer. Not all concepts can be employed on all viral videos, but the more concepts the more successful will the video get in a shorter amount of time, says Allocca. For an illustration he gives the example of the YouTube video "Yosemitebear Mountain Double Rainbow 1-8-10", a 3:29 minute long video of a man recording a double rainbow in the Yosemite Nationalpark. He even uploaded a lot of other nature videos, why did this video get over 39 million views so far? Here is how Allocca explains it: it was uploaded in January 2010, and was only picked up by masses of viewers when Jimmy Kimmel posted this video on Twitter. Allocca says, "Tastemakers like Jimmy Kimmel introduce us to new and interesting things and bring them to a larger audience". The community of participation here was Twitter, but it could have also been any other platform where Jimmy Kimmel might have been part of. This community participation makes us part of the phenomenon, it furthermore shapes the community, as already said, these are "in-group" features so that we feel connected and therefore we share it furthermore. The notion of unexpectedness, or surprise, is especially important when everyday two days of video is uploaded every minute; the content has to be exciting for the viewer, otherwise he/she will just close the video, never to return again. In the case of the Yosemitebear Mountain video, we as viewers not only see a double rainbow, but also hear to our surprise a ridiciously escalating man constantly saying "Woah", "wow", "oh (man)", "Yeeeaaah", "Woohoo" and making other sounds of astonishment. The viewer could get the impression this man has not ever seen a rainbow bearing in mind his excitement. This video has been so famous and so well-received by the community that the community got creative as well and made a parody video with the "Double Rainbow Song" which also gained over 34 million viewers.

What does it mean for us and our culture? Allocca argues that "tastemakers, creative participating communities, complete unexpectedness - these are characteristics of a new kind of media in a new kind of culture, where anyone has access and the audience defines the popularity". This will also define our future sense of entertainment. We share that video, because it is also a sign of being "in the group" - you understood that video, you thought it was funny, so you share it, which makes you smart and you are "in the know" (cf Konnikova 2014). These videos can through us, as sharers, even become part of our popular culture, in which we live and act.

ANALYSIS

According to previous studies on viral videos, the former chapter has argued that there are actual qualities that viral videos share that helped get them their huge success. The most common and relevant qualities mentioned by different authors were brevity, cuteness/charm, featuring funny people or animals (preferrably babies), the content does not need to be informative, but should have emotional content with a suprise factor, a headline that works as a link bait does help and a participating, creative audience.

This chapter will analyze four viral videos, looking for the qualities mentioned above and investigates if there are any similarities or differences in the videos. The videos chosen scored a huge success concerning viralness, all four list over 50 million views, and each will possess more than one of the qualities above.

"Charlie bit my finger - again!" The 55 second short video gained popularity within days and so far got over 670 million views internet-wide. The headline is very short and perfectly describes what happens within 55 seconds. While the two small British boys Harry and Charlie sit in an armchair and watch TV, Charlie is biting Harry's finger, then stops, Harry laughs and says "Ahaha Charlie. Charlie bit me" [00:00:04]. Then Harry puts his finger into his younger brother's mouth and of course Charlie bites Harry's finger very hard, which Harry first finds funny but then his face changes into an expression of pain. He screams "Ouch, Charlie" [00:00:28] and after some seconds Charlie lets go of Harry's finger. Harry retorts to Charlie with "Charlie, that really hurt" [00:00:30] but again after two seconds Harry's painful facial expression is gone and they both laugh. Harry then explains to Charlie "I'm not really hurt, but it is still hurting".

It was uploaded in 2006 but originally not for fun purposes or to get high popularity but rather to let a family member, who does not live nearby, see how the boys are doing. It scores with brevity as it does not take the viewer one minute to watch the whole video. The two British boys possess a huge load of cuteness, which Professor Cordell says "does well on the Internet", and they speak in a fine British accent, that almost sounds Posh, which does not hurt either. As Harry is only 3-years-old and Charlie just a baby they cover the aspect that funny people, especially babies, are very popular in the internet society.

To come to the suprise factor: within 55 seconds one might think that not too much can happen, this video is the proof that it can. It is not unexpected that babies like Charlie put everything in their mouth and bite on it, but what is unexpected is the fact that Harry puts his finger into Charlie's mouth again, although he knows from the experience ten seconds before that it will hurt. Again it is not unexpected that Harry then screams and is in pain, but it is surprising how Harry looks at Charlie, in total shock of what he did, but then calms down quickly, the pain vanishes from his face and he explains to Charlie that it did not "really" hurt. The viewer expects Harry to cry, which would be justified, but he is very understanding and calm which does not fit to his age.

Harry and Charlie are two very expressive children, especially Harry going from being passive first, to laughing, then screaming of pain, then being horrified of what Charlie did, and then laughs again. A lot of charm is involved as well as the viewer is emotionally taken away by Harry's cute British accent and by Charlie's laugh (cf Lyall 2012). Moreover is the video appealing, because it is real, and shows a small glimpse into an everyday life of a family.

The two boys have a very participating audience that did not hesitate to make parodies out of the video, for example did they replace Charlie with a zombie, or created several musicial remixes. The parodies are not as successful as the original but some even gained over 1 million views. Furthermore can they buy merchandise like t-shirts, which might also be a factor to get people "infected" by the video, but also to show connectivity.

"*The Sneezing Baby Panda*". This viral video is even shorter than "Charlie bit my finger - again!", consisting only of 16 seconds, gained over 191 million views and was uploaded in 2006 as well. It is still popular and still frequently watched, because the first comments left below the video are not even 14 hours old. Again the headline is very short consisting only of four words, and as it is only 16 seconds long it also possesses the qualitiy of brevity. It can be claimed that especially the word "Baby" attracts further viewers, because people enjoy watching babies, whether human or animal on the internet. What will get the viewer even more interested is the curiosity of how a panda acutally sneezes, especially how a baby panda sneezes.

The viewer is confronted with two pandas, the adult panda, probably the mother, eating and the baby panda lying silently at its feet. Despite the adult panda eating, and this is also the only thing we hear, nothing happens the first ten seconds, but the viewer of course suspects, already by reading the titlte, that something will happen and the suspense rises. In the eleventh second the baby panda sneezes, which gives the adult panda a fright and it jumps. The viewer in this scene is very likely to jump as well, because the sneeze is very loud and we did not expect it to be so loud, because two seconds before it was just lying there not making a noise. It is very rare that one gets to hear how a baby panda sneezes and the viewer is especially shocked to hear how loud it is and as already mentioned above videos that "shock or inspire are more likely to be shared . . . and more likely to gain viral traction" (Konnikova 2014). The adult panda gets the main attention at first, as it is the only thing that moves, and like the mother panda we are just as surprised as she is.

Ever since, the amount of sneezing animal videos and panda videos has risen, and there is even a parody featuring the sneeze as an explosion. YouTube even features a video of "Sneezing Baby Panda The Movie (2014) Official Trailer" which is based on the original internet phenomenon, telling the story of a zoo looking for the orginal sneezing baby panda, this is the proof that the video has an actively participating audience.

"Dramatic Chipmunk". Now to come to the shortest of the four videos, which consists of only five seconds and so far has over 40 million views and the parodies, GIFS, re-enactments or remixes are probably uncountable, featuring not only chipmunks but also rabbits, people, cats or eagles. In this five seconds we see a "chipmunk" standing with the back to us and all of a sudden it turns around while the camera zooms into its face and dramatic music is played. As it is one of the shortest viral videos it scores with brevity and also the headline consists only of two words. The viewer's interests is caught by the titel already of how a chipmunk can be dramatic or what it actually does to be dramatic so this works again as a link bait.

Due to the choice of dramatic music, the viewer somehow knows that something unusual is going to happen in between those five seconds, but it is probably not expected that a chipmunk has the ability to have a dramatic facial expression. This is the surprise factor of the video. Zatorre and Salimpoor describe in their article "Why Music Makes Our Brain Sing" how music produces emotional reactions and writes:

> ". . . each act of listening to music may be though of as both recapitulating the past and predicting the future. When we listen to music, these brain networks actively create expectations based on our stored knowledge"

The music used is *the* example for dramatic music which probably everyone knows and from earlier experiences our brain can predict what is most likely to happen. They claim ". . . performers intuitively understand this: they manipulate these prediction mechanisms to give us what we want - or to surprise us, perhaps even with something better.", which is exactly what the producers of this video did. We get surprised to what is going to happen (cf Zatorre,

Salimpoor 2013).

People still argue whether it is actually a chipmunk, a hamster or something else, but

experts have now revealed that it is rather a prairie dog. It was originally taken from a

Japanese TV Show and was uploaded afterwards on YouTube in 2007. The People Magazine

listed the video on "The 10 wildest YouTube Stars" in 2007, which could be argued to have

further more helped the video get viral success. As Kevin Allocca claims "Tastemakers" help

videos become viral and the People Magazine could be argued to be a tastemaker as it is rated

second place in the Top 10 Celebrity Magazines being very famous among its audience (cf

n.p. "Top 10 Celebrity Magazines").

"David After Dentist". This is probably the most diverse video compared to the other three

videos and gained so far over 120 million views. It consists of 1:58 minutes and is much

longer than the other three videos and therefore does not score with brevity. It was published

five years ago in 2009 by David's dad who wanted to tape his son for David's mother, who

could not come along when they went to the dentist. The headline is very short, consists only

of three words and already gives a hint to the viewer of what he or she is about to see. As

David just came from the surgery at the dentist, the viewer already expects something funny

to happen, maybe even gloating, because everyone knows how you feel after being on drugs.

This gets the viewer emotionally involved not only by their potential own experience, but

also are we somehow shocked and surprised about what David actually says. The father gets

David talking by asking him questions so the viewer gets more input of David, i.e. the father

makes it even funnier for the viewer.

Completely befuddled after the anaesthesia we watch David sitting in the back seat and almost philosophically asking his dad "Is this real life?" [00:00:18] and "I feel funny. Why is this happening to me?" [00:01:33]. As David proceeds with talking weird things, the viewer will find him very funny and laugh about what non-sense he is talking and about the way he gesticulates. At one second he screams and the other second he collapses into his seat, which does not make any sense at all and comes to no expectancy.

"David After Dentist" has a very participating and creative community, that contributed several parodies and remixes of the original. After the great success of the video many more videos named "X After Dentist" occurred on YouTube, but never one with the same success. The father created a homepage called davidafterdentist.com which is a blog and on which fans can buy merchandise like T-shirts.

CONCLUSION

From examining "Charlie bit my finger - again!", "The Sneezing Baby Panda", "David After Dentist" and "Dramatic Chipmunk" with special focus on what these four videos share and do not share, it is demonstrated that there are no universal qualities that will make videos automatically go viral, however were qualities found that might have helped get them this great success.

"Charlie bit my finger - again!", "The Sneezing Baby Panda" and "Dramatic Chipmunk" are very short ranging only from 5 seconds to 58 seconds, compared to "David After Dentist" which is rather "long" featuring 1:58 minutes. When looking at the amount of views, "Charlie bit my finger - again!" is in the lead with over 670 million clicks and the "Dramatic Chipmunk" in the end with "only" 40 million clicks, in the middle lying "David

After Dentist" with 120 million clicks, therefore it can not be claimed that the shorter the video the more viral it will get.

All videos had a suprise factor which sometimes shocked the viewer, but which was the essential part of the video. The viewer had expectancies which were triggered already by the short titles, but these expectancies were always exceeded. With "Charlie bit my finger - again!" it was Harry being so naive to put his finger back into Charlie's mouth, in the second video it was the surprise of how loud baby pandas actually sneeze, in the "Dramatic Chipmunk" it was the surprise of how dramatic a chipmunk (or prairie dog) can actually look and "David After Dentist" shocked the viewer and made him or her laugh about what funny things children can say when being on drugs. All this surprises got the viewer emotionally involved and got the viewer's attention to keep looking. When we look at the headlines, there seems to be a clear line, that they should be short and precise, so that the viewer can easily find and remember it.

There were no general or universal factors found in the four viral videos analyzed that could be claimed to predict their success. What was found were factors that made the video viewer-friendly, as for example short headlines that made it easy for the viewer to process the video. Viral videos that become even pop culture strongly depend on time, luck and on the viewer, whether he or she only watches it or decides to share it with friends via e-mail, blogs or a social website like Facebook, Reddit or Twitter. Each site has its own sharing behaviour, consisting of different preferences, which is also a cultural issue.

Works Cited

Alloca, Kevin. "Why videos go viral". *Ted.* November 2011. Video. 16 March 2014.

    [http://www.ted.com/talks/kevin_allocca_why_videos_go_viral]

Barret, Dan. "'Gangnam Style Holds Guiness World Record For Most 'Liked' Video in

    YouTube History". *Guinessworldrecords.* 20 September 2012. Web. 14 March 2014.

booba1234 [n.p.]. "David After Dentist". *YouTube.* 31 January 2009. Video. 17 March 2014.

cregets [n.p.]. "Dramatic Chipmunk". *YouTube.* 19 June 2007. Video. 17 March 2014.

HDCYT [n.p.]. "Charlie bit my finger - again!". *YouTube.* 22 May 2007. Video. 17 March

    2014.

jimvwmoss [n.p]. "The Sneezing Baby Panda." *YouTube.* 06 November 2011. Video. 17

    March 2014.

Keller, Jared. "The Secret to Going Viral: It's All About Culture". *The Atlantic.* 26 January

    2012. Web. 16 March 2014.

Konnikova, Maria. "The Six Things That Make Stories Go Viral Will Amaze, And Maybe

    Infuriate, You". *New Yorker.* 21 January 2014. Web. 16 March 2014.

Lehrer, Jonah. "Why Do Viral Videos Go Viral?". *Wired.* 25 July 2011. Web. 16 March 2014.

Lyall, Sarah. "417.6 Million Bites Later ...". *The New York Times.* 9 February 2012. Web. 18

    March 2014.

McCarthy, Carolin. "Five-second 'Dramatic Chipmunk' video takes the Web by storm".

    cnet.com. 22 June 2007. Web. 19 March 2014.

Miller, Claire Cain. "Cashing In on Your Hit YouTube Video". *The New York Times.* 26

    October 2011. Web. 17 March 2014.

Nalts, Kevin. "How Many Views Do You Need to Be Viral?". *willvideoforfood*. 6 May 2011.

Web. 17 March 2014.

Nobel, Carmen. "Advertising Symbiosis: The Key to Viral Videos". *Harvard Business*

School. 17 June 2013. Web. 17 March 2014.

O'Neill, Megan. "What Makes A Video 'Viral'". *SocialTimes*. 9 May 2011. Web. 17 March

2014.

Rosen, Rebecca J.. "The Viral-Media Prof Whose Kids Got 1 Million Facebook Likes (and a

Puppy)". *The Atlantic*. 19 January 2013. Web. 16 March 2014.

Seedwell Creative Studios. "The Edge: What Makes A Video Viral". *Seedwell*. 10 February

2012. Blog. 17 March 2014.

Thompson, Derek. "What's the Secret to Viral Success? It's So Obvious". *The Atlantic*. 27

June 2012. Web. 16 March 2014.

Zatorre, Robert J., Valorie N. Salimpoor. "Why Music makes Our Brain Sing". *The New York*

Times. 7 June 2013. Web. 19 March 2014.

n.p. "Jeden Tag sehen 10 Millionen Psy: Gangam Style bricht Rekorde". *n-tv.de*. 25

November 2012. Web. 14 March 2014.

n.p. "Top 10 Celebrity Magazines". *allyoucanread.com*. n.d. Web. 17 March 2014.

[http://www.allyoucanread.com/top-10-celebrity-magazines/]

YOUR KNOWLEDGE HAS VALUE

- We will publish your bachelor's and
  master's thesis, essays and papers

- Your own eBook and book -
  sold worldwide in all relevant shops

- Earn money with each sale

Upload your text at www.GRIN.com
and publish for free